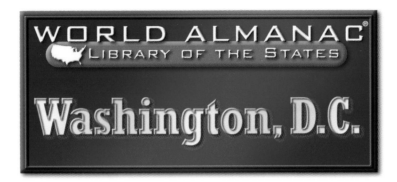

WORLD ALMANAC®
LIBRARY OF THE STATES

Washington, D.C.

by Acton Figueroa

WORLD ALMANAC® LIBRARY

Please visit our web site at: **www.worldalmanaclibrary.com**
For a free color catalog describing World Almanac® Library's list of high-quality books and multimedia programs, call 1-800-848-2928 (USA) or 1-800-387-3178 (Canada). World Almanac® Library's fax: (414) 332-3567.

Library of Congress Cataloging-in-Publication Data available upon request from publisher. Fax (414) 336-0157 for the attention of the Publishing Records Department.

ISBN 0-8368-5162-5 (lib. bdg.)
ISBN 0-8368-5333-4 (softcover)

First published in 2003 by
World Almanac® Library
330 West Olive Street, Suite 100
Milwaukee, WI 53212 USA

Copyright © 2003 by World Almanac® Library.

A Creative Media Applications Production
Design: Alan Barnett, Inc.
Copy editor: Laurie Lieb
Fact checker: Joan Verniero
Photo researcher: Jamey O'Quinn
World Almanac® Library project editor: Tim Paulson
World Almanac® Library editors: Mary Dykstra, Gustav Gedatus, Jacqueline Laks Gorman, Lyman Lyons
World Almanac® Library art direction: Tammy Gruenewald
World Almanac® Library graphic designers: Scott M. Krall, Melissa Valuch

Photo credits: pp. 4-5 © Getty Images; p. 6 (bottom) © AP/Wide World Photos; p. 6 (top) © PhotoDisc/Getty Images; p. 7 (top and bottom) © AP/Wide World Photos; p. 9 © Hulton Archive/Getty Images; p. 10 © Hulton Archive/Getty Images; p. 11 © Hulton Archive/Getty Images; p. 12 © Hulton Archive/Getty Images; p. 13 © Hulton Archive/Getty Images; p. 14 © AP/Wide World Photos; p. 15 © AP/Wide World Photos; p. 16 © AP/Wide World Photos; p. 17 © AP/Wide World Photos; p. 18 © Royalty-Free/CORBIS; p. 19 © Hulton Archive/Getty Images; p. 20 (left) © PhotoDisc/Getty Images; p. 20 (center) © AP/Wide World Photographs; p. 20 (right) © AP/Wide World Photos; p. 21 (left) © AP/Wide World Photos; p. 21 (center) © AP/Wide World Photos; p. 21 (right) © AP/Wide World Photos; p. 23 © AP/Wide World Photos; p. 25 © Royalty-Free/CORBIS; p. 26 © Royalty-Free/CORBIS; p. 29 © AP/Wide World Photos; p. 30 © AP/Wide World Photos; p. 31 © AP/Wide World Photos; p. 32 © Royalty-Free/CORBIS; p. 33 © AP/Wide World Photos; p. 34 © AP/Wide World Photos; p. 35 © AP/Wide World Photos; p. 36 © AP/Wide World Photos; p. 37 (top) © AP/Wide World Photos; p. 37 (bottom) © AP/Wide World Photos; 38 © Hulton Archive/Getty Images; 39 (left) © Hulton Archive/Getty Images; 39 (right) © AP/Wide World Photos; 40 (top) © AP/Wide World Photos; 40 (bottom) © AP/Wide World Photos; 41 © AP/Wide World Photos; pp. 42-43 © Hulton Archive/Getty Images; p. 44 (top and bottom) © AP/Wide World Photos; p. 45 (top and bottom) © AP/Wide World Photos

Printed in the United States of America

1 2 3 4 5 6 7 8 9 07 06 05 04 03

Washington, D.C.

The Nation's Capital

Washington, D.C., is the capital of the United States. Visitors to the capital need only look around to see symbols of this country's past. The Washington Monument is a tribute to the man called "the father of our country." The Lincoln Memorial has placed a statue of the man who freed the slaves facing the Capitol, so he can keep a watchful eye on those who govern this country. The Korean War Veterans Memorial, the Vietnam Veterans Memorial, and the Vietnam Women's Memorial are testaments to those who died fighting for their country in those wars.

But Washington, D.C., is more than just a symbol of the past. It is also the seat of the national government. It is home to the president and the cabinet, to the U.S. Senate, and the U.S. House of Representatives. Here, the U.S. Supreme Court meets to make decisions that affect us all.

Finally, Washington, D.C., is a city in its own right, an exciting metropolis with more than half a million residents. It is home to world-class museums, respected educational foundations, and corporate headquarters for international businesses. It is also home to seventeen colleges and universities, embassies representing countries from around the world, and what is perhaps the greatest metropolitan transit system in existence. Because it has so many attractions, Washington, D.C., is a destination for U.S. citizens and visitors from foreign countries. Tourists come to explore this great city, enjoy its famous music and art, and learn about the history of the United States.

Washington, D.C., is a place that means different things to different people. It is thought of as the seat of our government, a fantastic place to visit, and a place to work or go to school. Most importantly, it is a lasting symbol of our country's thriving democracy.

▶ Map of the Washington, D.C., area showing the interstate highway system, as well as waterways and neighboring cities and towns.

▼ Red, white, and blue balloons decorate the sky over the Capitol.

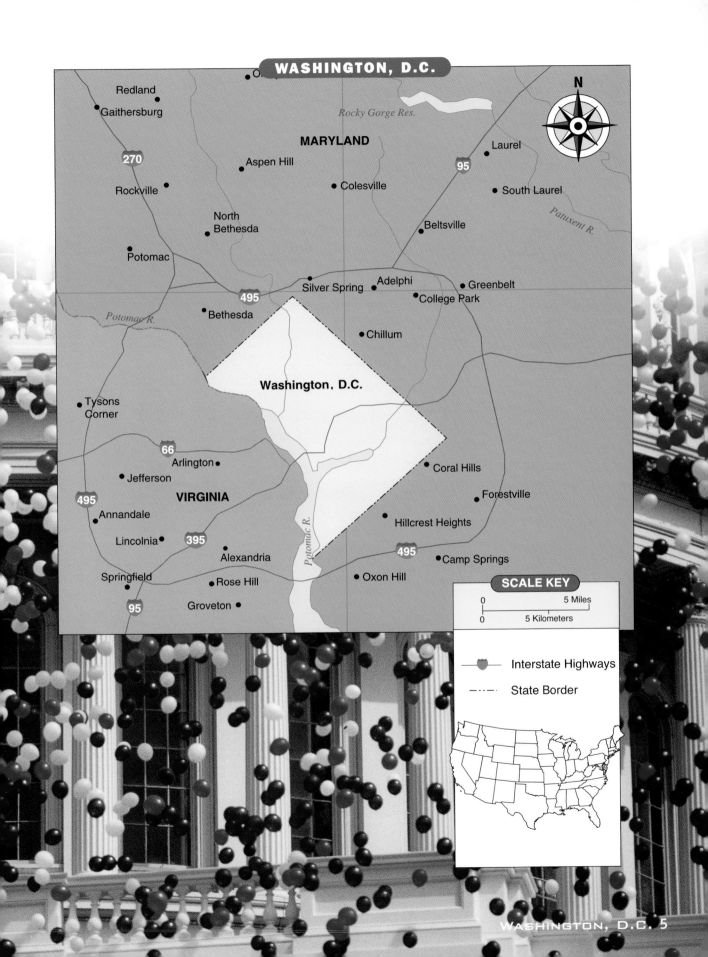

N

Redland

Gaithersburg

Rocky Gorge Res.

MARYLAND

270

Aspen Hill

Laurel

95

Colesville

Rockville

South Laurel

North
Bethesda

Patuxent R.

Beltsville

Potomac

495

Silver Spring

Adelphi

Greenbelt

College Park

Potomac R.

Bethesda

Chillum

Washington, D.C.

Tysons
Corner

66

Arlington

Coral Hills

Jefferson

Forestville

VIRGINIA

495

Hillcrest Heights

Annandale

Lincolnia

395

Potomac R.

495

Alexandria

Camp Springs

Springfield

Oxon Hill

Rose Hill

95

Groveton

SCALE KEY

0   5 Miles

0   5 Kilometers

Interstate Highways

- · - · - · - State Border

Fast Facts

Washington, D.C.

Designated as U.S. Capital

1791

Total Population (2000)

572,059 — *Between 1990 and 2000, the city's population decreased 5.7 percent.*

Land Area

61 square miles (158 square kilometers)

Motto

Justitia Omnibus — *Latin for "Justice to all"*

Bird

Wood thrush — *Distinguished by its reddish-brown head and neck and white chest, it also has pink legs and a white ring around its eyes. The wood thrush's song sounds like a flute.*

Flower

American Beauty rose — *Famous for its strong fragrance, deep pink, crimson color, and cupped double petals. This rose has been a favorite for years.*

Tree

Scarlet oak — *A medium to large tree, the scarlet oak's leaves have red stems and flared points. Its round acorns are an important food source for larger birds and mammals.*

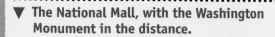

▼ **The National Mall, with the Washington Monument in the distance.**

PLACES TO VISIT

The Constitution Gardens
Situated on more than 50 acres (20 hectares) of land, these gardens are in the middle of the city. Army engineers dredged the Potomac River to create them. An annual ceremony is held here to honor new citizens.

National Aquarium
The nation's oldest aquarium is filled with a variety of marine creatures — sharks, eels, sea turtles, and dolphins — and is an exciting place for visitors of all ages. Highlights include animal feedings, educational talks, and more than twelve hundred types of aquatic life.

The National Museum of Women's History
Learn about women who shaped the history of the world. Exhibits feature notable women from astronauts and spies to suffragettes and sports figures.

For other places and events, see p. 44.

BIGGEST, BEST, AND MOST

- Washington, D.C., is home to the most African Americans with college degrees in the U.S.

- The Washington Monument is the tallest masonry structure in the world at 555 feet, 5 inches (169.3 m).

- The Corcoran Gallery of Art is the oldest and largest private art museum in the United States.

WASHINGTON, D.C., FIRSTS

- 1784 James Ramsey tested his new invention, the first steam-powered motorboat.

- 1880 Gallaudet University opened the area's first indoor swimming pool, the second in the United States.

- 1895 President Grover Cleveland was the first U.S. president to appear in a film. He was filmed signing a bill into law, and the footage appeared in *A Capital Courtship*.

Famous First Ladies

From Martha Washington onward, presidential wives handled their position in a variety of ways. Not all of them were entirely happy with their situations. Martha Washington spoke for many future first ladies when she said, "I think I am more like a state prisoner than anything else." First Lady Eleanor Roosevelt wrote a daily newspaper column and traveled the country. Jacqueline Kennedy organized a restoration of the White House. Hillary Rodham Clinton chaired the National Task Force on Health Care Reform. As a former teacher and librarian, Laura Bush has made reading a national priority. Her program "Ready to Read, Ready to Learn" highlights the importance of starting children on the road to reading at an early age.

A Capital Wonder — the Metro

With the many amazing sights to see in Washington, D.C., one sight never fails to make visitors gasp: the subway system, or Metro. Construction on the Metro began in 1969, and the first phase was opened in 1976. Today, the Metro carries 650,000 passengers daily, funneling them through its cavernous, cathedral-like stations onto practically silent trains that run on rubber wheels. With eighty-three stations and 103 miles (166 kilometers) of track, the Metro is the best way to get around the city.

The City on the Potomac

America has furnished to the world the character of Washington. And if our American institutions had done nothing else, that alone would have entitled them to the respect of mankind.

— *Daniel Webster, on the completion of the Bunker Hill Monument, June 17, 1843*

The earliest known settlers of the area that is now Washington, D.C., were the Piscataway Native Americans. This group had one large village on Piscataway Creek in Maryland, as well as approximately thirty smaller settlements. Among these smaller settlements was Nacochtank, a name that was later changed by European settlers to Anacostia. According to *Relatio*, a written account by a Jesuit missionary named Father White, the Piscataway fished in the Potomac River, harvested shellfish, and cultivated corn, pumpkins, and tobacco in the rich soil. The Piscataway lived in shared homes of bark, with a central fire in each. These structures were built with holes in the roof to allow smoke to vent, in a manner similar to a chimney. The Piscataway seem to have had an organized social structure, with men of importance being given special sleeping platforms, while common people slept on the floors of the buildings. The original population of the Piscataway has been estimated at twenty-five hundred people.

English Settlement

European settlers arrived in the early 1600s. In 1608, Captain John Smith sailed up the Potomac and met with members of the Piscataway at Nacochtank. This meeting was friendly; later encounters between the Natives and settlers would not be. By the time fur trapper Henry Fleete arrived in 1632, the Piscataway had established comfortable relations with several Catholic missionaries in the area. By the middle of the seventeenth century, however, more Europeans arrived and disputes over land

Native Americans of Washington, D.C.

Piscataway

DID YOU KNOW?

Washington, D.C., has had several names. While it was being built, people called it "the Federal City." When it was offically founded, or incorporated, in 1800, it was named Washington. But because the United States was sometimes called "Columbia" in the eighteenth century (after Christopher Columbus), Washington was given the additional name of "District of Columbia," or D.C.

erupted. Many members of the Piscataway died from smallpox, a deadly disease brought by the Europeans; others died in battle with the settlers and other Native tribes. By 1697, the Piscataway had fewer than four hundred members.

The king of England, James I, in the hopes of colonizing the New World, granted a charter to the Virginia Company of London. In 1607, this company sent 105 people in three ships to the New World. They established the first settlement at Jamestown that year. In 1618, George Yeardley was appointed colonial governor of Virginia. He set up the first representative legislature in the colonies in 1619, the Virginia House of Burgess. Together with this new legislative group, Governor Yeardley established laws for the people of the colony. In 1624, King James I declared Virginia a royal colony and sent his own governor to rule. The government may have changed, but the hard living conditions had not. Diseases such as smallpox, yellow fever, measles, and the bubonic plague were common, and infant mortality was high.

In 1652, Oliver Cromwell helped overthrow King Charles I in the English civil war. In the years that followed, the British struggled to exercise control over the colonies. After the conclusion of the French and Indian War in 1763, the British government tried to make the North American

DID YOU KNOW?

When Pierre-Charles L'Enfant designed the capital, he envisioned a city with enough space for what seemed an unusually large number of people to comfortably live and work. At the time, there were only three million people in all of the thirteen colonies. L'Enfant's papers state that he based his plans on the idea that the city would someday number eight hundred thousand people!

▼ In 1607, the village of Jamestown on the James River became the first permanent English settlement in America.

colonies pay higher taxes. The colonists thought these taxes were unfair. The taxes, along with the colonists' lack of representation in the British government, led to fighting in 1775. On July 4, 1776, the Continental Congress approved the Declaration of Independence, which announced the separation of the colonies from England. Intense battles between the British and U.S. troops continued until 1781. In 1783, the Treaty of Paris was signed, and the United States won the battle for freedom.

Planning the New Capital

Immediately after the war, the new country was without a capital. Philadelphia served as a temporary capital during the war, but the Southern states objected to this, because Philadelphia had a great many Quaker citizens. Quakers were vehemently opposed to slavery, which was already a part of the economic life in the South. Thus, even before the country had a capital, the conflict that would tear the country apart in the 1860s had begun. Finally, in 1789, Thomas Jefferson, a statesman who would be elected the third president, and Alexander Hamilton, the secretary of the treasury, came to an agreement that the capital should be located in the South. In order for Hamilton, a Northerner, to

▼ This 1880 map of Washington shows the completed city with its broad boulevards, tree-lined streets, and government buildings laid out in a grid pattern.

agree to this, the Southern states had to agree to allow the federal government to create taxes to pay the Revolutionary War debt.

Shortly after the decision was announced, Pierre-Charles L'Enfant, a French engineer, artist, and architect who had served in the Continental Army, wrote to President Washington. L'Enfant explained that he wanted to create a city that would be a symbol of the greatness of its nation. To Washington, who loved the chosen area's natural beauty and had fought long and hard to found the United States, this must have been an attractive proposition. In 1791, the president appointed L'Enfant chief engineer and planner for the capital city. This would turn out to be a wise choice, for his plans were magnificent.

L'Enfant designed a city of wide boulevards extending from the Capitol. One such boulevard, Pennsylvania Avenue, leads directly to the White House. It was during the construction of these boulevards that L'Enfant encountered a problem that would lead to his being fired. A large house was being built by an influential citizen directly in the path of a planned avenue. When L'Enfant had the house torn down, even though the owner had not given his permission, he was dismissed. He was replaced by an engineer named Andrew Ellicott. Ellicott respected L'Enfant's ideas and worked as closely as possible to his original plans.

It took years to build the nation's capital. In 1792, the first stone was laid for the White House, then called the President's House. One year later, construction began on the Capitol.

The White House was not completed when John Adams took office in 1797. He didn't move into the White House until 1800. That same year, the city was incorporated as Washington, in honor of the first president, and the employees of the federal government, mainly clerks and officials, moved to the city.

Benjamin Banneker

When L'Enfant was fired and returned to Paris, he took his designs for Washington, D.C., with him. The job of re-creating these plans in a way that would please L'Enfant's critics fell to engineer Andrew Ellicott, who was assisted by Benjamin Banneker, one of the country's best surveyors. Banneker, a free black farmer, had only a few months of formal schooling, but his math skills and ability to use delicate instruments enabled him to publish astronomical almanacs. Banneker was working on an almanac when Ellicott, a family friend, asked for his help in laying out the proposed city. Joining Ellicott in this job, Banneker helped give Washington, D.C., its organized structure. Banneker died in 1806.

The Early Years

From the very beginning, Washington, D.C., was a racially integrated city. As early as 1810, approximately one-third the city's population was African American. Free blacks, African Americans who had been born to a free mother or bought or received their freedom from their owners, settled in the capital in great numbers. In 1830, about twelve thousand African Americans lived in Washington, D.C., and approximately half of them were free.

The early years of the capital were full of upheaval. There was little money to spend on construction or public works, so important buildings such as the Treasury and the Capitol were built very slowly, and the streets remained unpaved.

In 1814, however, the fate of the new country and the still unfinished capital were both in danger. The United States had declared war on Great Britain in 1812, and in August of 1814, more than four thousand British troops landed in Maryland and marched to Washington. Panicked citizens packed their belongings and fled the city.

When the British troops arrived, they found the city empty. They set the White House, the Capitol, and several other government buildings on fire. The new capital was in great danger. It had been only thirty-one years since the United States had won its independence from the British, and now

▼ The British attacked the new American capital during the War of 1812. The assault took place on August 24, 1814.

the country was on the verge of collapse. Both the country and the capital would survive, however. A heavy rainstorm put out the fires in the city, and the country ended its war with Britain in 1815. Work on the heavily damaged White House was completed in 1817. It would be five years, however, before the Capitol was ready to hold a session of Congress.

The Civil War

The first fifty years of the nineteenth century were a mix of good and bad. The War of 1812 was costly and destructive, but the country continued to grow. The United States soon extended from the Atlantic Ocean to the Pacific Ocean, and the city of Washington had grown to forty thousand people by 1850.

Even as the United States prospered, however, a crucial problem would put its survival in danger. Slavery, seen by Southerners as necessary to their economic survival, was viewed as morally wrong by the Northern states and most of the world. In Washington, a meeting place for representatives of every state in the Union, the situation was becoming heated. Members of Congress argued over slavery, and at times the arguments led to actual fist fights. An act of Congress in 1850 made the buying and selling of slaves in Washington, D.C., illegal, but the owning of slaves remained legal. This act, the Compromise Act of 1850, was seen as a way to ease the tensions between the North and the South. It did not work.

When Abraham Lincoln was elected president in 1860, he knew that the issue of slavery had to be addressed. Lincoln was widely disliked in the South, as his antislavery stance was well known there. However, he had no plans to abolish slavery. The South did not believe this, and on April 12, 1861, Confederate troops fired the first shots of the Civil War on Fort Sumter, South Carolina.

The war between the North and the South lasted until 1865. At one point, Southern troops came within 4 miles (6.4 km) of the White House. Life in the capital changed during these years. The Capitol was used as a hospital for wounded soldiers. During the war, President Lincoln signed the Emancipation Proclamation, freeing the slaves in the Confederate states. As escaped slaves poured into the city, the population rose to 120,000.

▲ This photograph from 1865 shows the box at Ford's Theatre where President Lincoln was assassinated.

Lincoln's Assassination

On April 14, 1865, President and Mrs. Lincoln attended a performance at Ford's Theatre. Actor John Wilkes Booth slipped behind Lincoln and shot him in the head. Booth was a supporter of slavery who had previously plotted to kidnap Lincoln. The president was carried to the home of William Peterson, a tailor; Lincoln died the following morning. A witness, Edward M. Thornton, said of Lincoln, "Now he belongs to the ages."

Confederate general Robert E. Lee surrendered on April 9, 1865. The South had nearly been destroyed, but the Northern states had won an important moral victory. There was little time to celebrate this victory, however. On April 14, 1865, President Lincoln was assassinated. Once again, the capital of the United States was shadowed by tragedy.

As it had after the War of 1812, the city rose to the occasion. The postwar years were marked by the completion of many important buildings and monuments in the city, among them the Washington Monument, the State, War, and Navy building, the Library of Congress, and the Smithsonian Institution's Arts and Industries building. In 1867, the Freedmen's Bureau helped found Howard University — to this day, one of the country's finest predominantly African-American colleges.

▲ Its five-sided shape gave the Pentagon its name. (The prefix *penta-* means "five.")

The Twentieth Century

The first half of the twentieth century was marked by both international and domestic crises. The United States entered World War I in 1917; the war ended one year later. The 1920s saw a booming economy followed by the economic crash of 1929. The Great Depression that followed was a difficult time for the nation. President Franklin D. Roosevelt's New Deal, a program designed to give economic relief to the unemployed and revitalize industry, brought thousands of new government employees into the city. Even as Roosevelt's programs brought a measure of stability to the country, segregation (the separation of races) remained a problem.

When the United States was attacked by Japan on December 7, 1941, the country entered World War II. The year 1945 saw both the death of President Roosevelt and the end of the war. After the war, many white residents of the capital began to move to the suburbs. As a result, African Americans were in the majority by the mid-1950s.

The 1960 election saw President John F. Kennedy bring his youthful energy, commitment to desegregation, and opposition to nuclear weapons to Washington, D.C. The nation would soon weather crises such as the botched Bay of Pigs invasion in Cuba and the Cuban missile crisis. During Kennedy's presidency, Martin Luther King, Jr. delivered his famous "I Have a Dream" speech, at a Civil Rights rally of more than 200,000 people. A few months later, Kennedy's term in office ended with his assassination. Once again, the nation mourned a fallen leader.

The late 1960s and 1970s were also difficult for the nation and its capital. The assassinations of Martin Luther King, Jr. and presidential candidate Robert Kennedy; the Vietnam War; the Watergate scandal; and an economic recession lowered morale. Washington, D.C., suffered greatly, with a high crime rate and a faltering city government. However, the nation remained as interested as ever in the personalities and intrigues of its leaders, from Ronald Reagan and his folksy speeches in the 1980s to the scandals of Bill Clinton's administration in the 1990s.

The beginning of the twenty-first century brought yet another tragedy to the Washington area. On September 11, 2001, a jet hijacked by terrorists crashed into the Pentagon, one of four jets hijacked that day. One-hundred-twenty-five U.S. employees were killed at the Pentagon. Again, the nation looked to its capital for guidance during this, one of the worst crises in the nation's history.

Helen Thomas, Journalist

Born in 1920, Helen Thomas broke through many of the barriers that stood in the way of female journalists. In 1943, she began working for United Press International in Washington, D.C., writing news reports for the radio. In 1955, she began covering the Department of Justice, including the FBI. She eventually began attending presidential press conferences and briefings, where her straightforward questions and no-nonsense attitude distinguished her from other reporters. Thomas was the only journalist to travel with President Nixon on his visit to China in 1972, and since then, she has traveled the world with Presidents Nixon, Ford, Carter, Reagan, and George H. W. Bush.

Below: Journalist Helen Thomas (front) helps unveil the Women in Journalism stamps during a ceremony marking the stamps' first day of issue. Thomas paved the way for women interested in print and broadcast journalism.

Citizens of the Capital

> If a man hasn't discovered something that
> he will die for, he isn't fit to live.
>
> — *Dr. Martin Luther King, Jr. speech in Detroit, June 23, 1963*

There are slightly fewer than 600,000 people living within the city limits of Washington, D.C., making it the twenty-first largest U.S. city. The population in 1950 was 802,178. In the years between 1950 and 2000, many factors caused people to move out to the surrounding suburbs. Like people across the country in the years after World War II, Washingtonians felt that life in the suburbs would be preferable to an urban life. This migration was predominantly white, however, because at that time, most suburbs remained unofficially segregated. As a result, the city of Washington, D.C., would eventually have a majority of African-American citizens.

Age Distribution in Washington, D.C.
(2000 Census)

0–4	32,536
5–19	103,270
20–24	51,823
25–44	189,439
45–64	125,093
65 & over	69,898

▼ Many people who work in Washington, D.C., live in suburbs such as Arlington, Virginia.

Patterns of Immigration

The total number of people who immigrated to Washington, D.C., in 1998 was 2,337. Of that number, the largest immigrant groups were from El Salvador (18.3%), Nigeria (5.3%), and China (4.8%).

Ethnicities

The first non-Native people to live in the area now known as Washington, D.C., were European settlers. Because it was formed from land taken from Virginia and Maryland, both slaveholding states, Washington, D.C., had a large African-American population from the very beginning. When President Lincoln freed the slaves, many former slaves moved to the city from surrounding states. The African-American population is currently about 60 percent of the city's total. Approximately 30 percent of the population is Caucasian. In the nineteenth century, when most cities experienced a rapid growth in numbers of immigrants from northern and eastern European countries, Washington, D.C.'s population remained relatively stable. Because it did not have an industry (like the factories of the Northeast) that could absorb large numbers of workers, most of the immigrants chose to go elsewhere.

Small numbers of Italian and eastern European Jewish communities formed, but for the most part, the descendants of these groups left the city for the suburbs in the 1950s. A small Chinese community formed during the nineteenth century as well, settling along Pennsylvania Avenue. In the 1930s, when new federal office buildings were needed, this group was forced to move to a new location in the city.

▲ Thousands of Washington citizens joined the Civil Rights Movement in 1963 and crowded the Mall to hear Martin Luther King, Jr. give his "I Have a Dream" speech.

DID YOU KNOW?

Washington, D.C., has a high concentration of professionals. There are more doctors, lawyers, dentists, and psychiatrists per capita (per person) in the capital than any other city in the country.

Heritage and Background, Washington, D.C.   Year 2000

▶ Here is a look at the racial backgrounds of Washingtonians today.

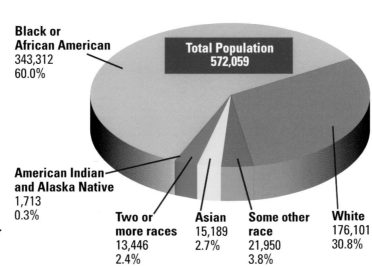

Black or African American
343,312
60.0%

Total Population
572,059

Note: 7.9% (44,953) of the population identify themselves as **Hispanic** or **Latino,** a cultural designation that crosses racial lines. Hispanics and Latinos are counted in this category as well as the racial category of their choice.

American Indian and Alaska Native
1,713
0.3%

Native Hawaiian and Other Pacific Islander
348
0.1%

Two or more races
13,446
2.4%

Asian
15,189
2.7%

Some other race
21,950
3.8%

White
176,101
30.8%

Religion

Most Washingtonians are of Protestant Christian faith. Baptists, Methodists, and Episcopalians are among the largest groups. Roman Catholics and Jews are also represented in the population. There are many churches in the capital, among them the Cathedral Church of Saint Peter and Saint Paul. Located in the Northwest section of the city, the National Cathedral, as it is commonly called, is the sixth-largest cathedral in the world. President Jefferson worshipped at Christ Church, an Episcopalian church in the Southeast section that is still standing and active two hundred years later. President Lincoln worshipped at New York Avenue Presbyterian Church during his presidency. One hundred years later, President Kennedy worshipped at the Cathedral of Saint Matthew the Apostle.

Educational Levels of Washington, D.C., Workers (age 25 and over)	
Less than 9th grade	29,803
9th to 12th grade, no diploma	55,446
High school graduate, including equivalency	79,169
Some college, no degree or associate degree	69,880
Bachelor's degree	69,496
Graduate or professional degree	80,741

▼ The Gothic-style National Cathedral is among the many architecturally impressive structures in Washington, D.C.

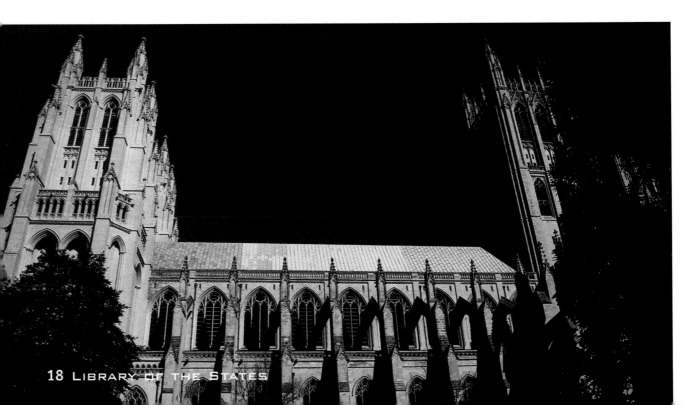

Education

With eighty thousand students currently enrolled, the public school system in Washington, D.C., is relatively small. As of 2002, there were 169 schools in the district. Before 1954, the public schools were segregated. In that year, the U.S. Supreme Court ruled that racial segregation was unconstitutional. After the ruling, the schools were integrated, with the result that many middle-class white families chose to place their children in private schools. The integration of the school system did gradually improve conditions for all public school students, but by the late twentieth century, the system was clearly struggling. The high school dropout rate is one of the highest in the nation, and 65 percent of students test below their grade level. The school system does offer options, however, such as magnet schools that have special academic programs for students showing aptitude in a particular subject.

In contrast to the troubled public school system, higher education flourishes in Washington, D.C. The largest university in the capital, The George Washington University, has twenty thousand students. The University of the District of Columbia, founded in 1974, has three campuses across the city. It offers associate degrees, bachelor's degrees, and master's degrees, as well as courses designed to upgrade the job skills of district residents. Father John Carroll founded the nation's oldest Catholic university, Georgetown, in 1789. Highly respected Howard University, one of the best-known predominantly African-American universities in the country, was founded in 1867 and has been attracting African Americans to the capital ever since. Howard offers many exciting activities and organizations to its students. The university has a long history of fraternity life; six of the nine national African-American fraternities originated at Howard in the early 1900s. Currently, Howard has both fraternities and sororities that serve to introduce students to new people, as well as encourage them to participate in worthwhile programs and services that benefit the community.

▲ As shown in this 1940 photo, the football huddle started at Gallaudet University to prevent other teams from reading the sign language used by its deaf players.

Gallaudet University

In 1864, the first eight students enrolled in the National College for the Deaf and the Dumb (mute), after President Lincoln signed a bill into law allowing the college to grant degrees to deaf students. Since that time, the college, now known as Gallaudet University, has continued to educate deaf students in the district as well as at seven regional centers around the country. In 1988, the university appointed its first deaf president, Dr. I. King Jordan.

Along the Potomac

> A nation may be said to consist of its territory, its people, and its laws. The territory is the only part which is of certain durability.
>
> — *Abraham Lincoln, second annual message to Congress, December 1, 1862*

Washington, D.C., although known throughout the world as the seat of power of the United States, covers a relatively small area — just 61 square miles (158 sq km). The border of the District of Columbia lies along the Potomac River to the southeast.

The Mighty Potomac

The river that defines the city of Washington, D.C., originates in the Allegheny Mountains of West Virginia. Several tributaries combine to make one large river in Maryland. The Potomac drains an area of approximately 14,500 square miles (37,555 sq km). The river, flowing through the city and into Chesapeake Bay, supplies fresh drinking and household water to 80 percent of the residents of the greater Washington, D.C., area, a population of four million. The Anacostia River flows into the Potomac in Washington, D.C.

The development of the city and the surrounding suburbs has had a negative effect on the water quality of the Potomac and the animal life in the area. Organizations

Highest Point
Tenleytown
410 feet (125 meters) above sea level

▼ *From left to right:* **The Hirshhorn Museum; cherry blossoms and the Washington Monument; biking along the Potomac; a tall ship sails near the Capitol; Hsing-Hsing, the National Zoo's male panda; the view from the Anacostia neighborhood near Martin Luther King, Jr. Avenue.**

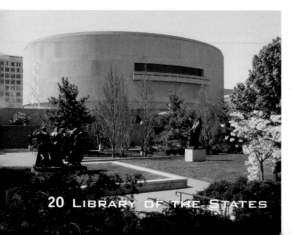

like the Potomac Conservancy are working to protect the river and its inhabitants. The Conservancy has begun a land protection program to prevent the wetlands from being destroyed, and it works to clean and restore the water of the river, while providing support for more than seventy other groups working toward the same goals.

Rock Creek Park

Rock Creek Park was acquired by the city of Washington in 1890. At 1,754 acres (710 ha), it is one of the largest natural parks within city limits anywhere in the world. It has more than 15 miles (24 km) of hiking trails, abundant natural wildlife (for an urban setting), a variety of flowering plants and trees, and Rock Creek, a body of water that runs through the northwest part of the city. Within the park is the Battleground National Cemetery, where forty-one soldiers who died in the Civil War Battle of Fort Stevens are buried. This is one of the smallest national cemeteries in the country. The Pierce Mill, a water-powered mill that was in operation until 1897, now serves as a museum and a ranger station. The park has been a popular destination for tourists since it opened.

Plants and Animals

For an urban setting, Washington, D.C., has a fairly wide array of wildlife. The Potomac and its branches are host to a variety of fish, including shad, sunfish, catfish, and bass. On its banks nest the great blue heron and the bald eagle. The vast acreage of Rock Creek Park is home to deer, squirrels, chipmunks, and foxes.

Like any city, the capital is home to thousands of pigeons. Oddly, considering that the district is an inland city, it is also home to large flocks of seagulls. Other birds that call Washington, D.C., home are thrushes, warblers,

| Average January temperature 35°F (2°C) |
| Average July temperature 79°F (26°C) |
| Average yearly rainfall 39 inches (99 cm) |
| Average yearly snowfall 16 inches (41 cm) |

DID YOU KNOW?

The lowest point in Washington, D.C., is the Potomac River, which is near sea level.

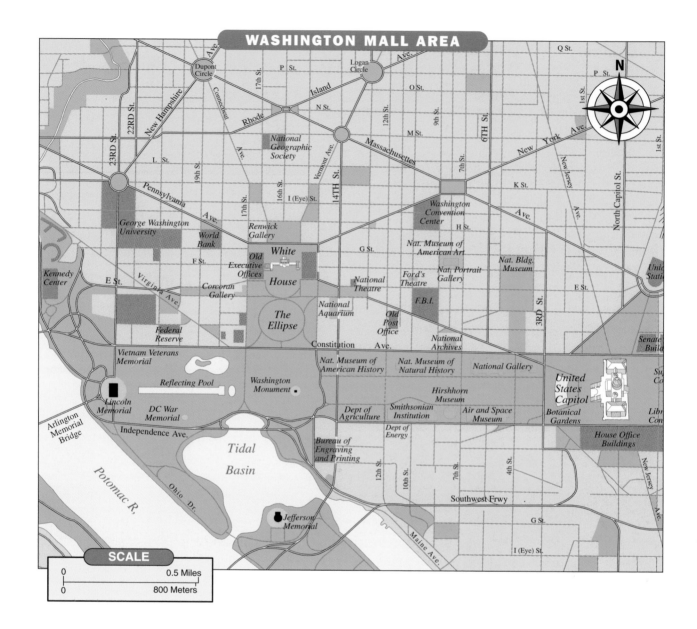

SCALE

| 0 | 0.5 Miles |
| 0 | 800 Meters |

and finches. Bird watching is a popular activity for Washingtonians, which makes sense when one considers that the Audubon Society is located in nearby Maryland.

The hospitable climate and long growing season in Washington, D.C., have added greatly to its natural beauty. When the developers of the city chopped down the existing trees, new ones were planted that kept with L'Enfant's carefully planned boulevards. Poplar trees, lindens, oaks, and sycamores now grow along the majestic avenues. The capital's best known trees are its cherry trees, originally a gift from Japan in the early twentieth century. The National Arboretum, a park of 444 acres (180 ha), is planted with flowering trees and shrubs, including dogwoods, azaleas, and magnolias.

The Capital's Neighborhoods

Washington, D.C., is divided into four unequal sections. The boundaries of these four sections intersect at the Capitol. The Northwest section includes the White House, several of the Smithsonian buildings, and the Lincoln Memorial. Five universities, fine restaurants and hotels, and the neighborhoods of Georgetown and Dupont Circle are in the Northeast section. The Northeast section is also home to the Catholic University of America, and the National Arboretum. The Southeast section includes both the Anacostia neighborhood, an area of run-down homes, and new developments near the Capitol. The Southwest section is the smallest. By the 1940s, this section was considered to be a slum, but as a result of urban renewal in the 1960s, the neighborhood has been transformed into a mix of modern buildings and open spaces. The National Mall separates the Southwest from the Northwest section.

▼ In spring, cherry trees, a gift from Japan, bloom along the Potomac River. The Jefferson Memorial, which is surrounded by cherry trees, is the centerpiece of the annual Cherry Blossom Festival.

The Big Business of Government

> Washington, D.C., is a city of Southern
> efficiency and Northern charm.
> — *John F. Kennedy, quoted in Arthur Schlesinger's*
> A Thousand Days

There are several industries in Washington, but they are all linked to one single industry that runs the nation — the federal government. Of the more than one-quarter million employed people over the age of sixteen in the year 2000, more than one in four worked for the government. The second largest industry after the federal government is tourism, made up of the transportation companies, hotels, restaurants, and other companies and organizations that provide hospitality to the millions of people who visit Washington, D.C., every year. A large percentage of the rest of the workers are employed by companies that either support the people who work in the government — the banks, realtors, and service people — or by companies that seek to influence the government in some way. Many social welfare organizations, financial organizations, and cultural organizations are located in Washington, D.C.

The Federal Government

From the 126 clerks who moved to Washington, D.C., in November 1800, the number of federal employees has grown to almost 40,000 workers. As many as 15 percent of the adults employed in the district are federal government employees. Although this percentage seems high, it is down from the year 1940, when 44 percent of the population was employed by the federal government. From the president to the people who run the cafeteria in the Senate building, federal employees keep Washington, D.C., running.

Top Employers (of workers age sixteen and over)	
Services	55.2%
Federal, state, and local government (including military)	15.0
Transportation, communications, and public utilities	10.0%
Finance, insurance, and real estate	7.4%
Wholesale and retail trade	6.9%
Construction	3.9%
Manufacturing	1.5%
Agriculture, forestry, fishing and hunting, and mining	0.1%

▲ Tourists come to Washington, D.C., from all over the world. Above, visitors approach the National Gallery of Art to enjoy its collection of paintings, sculpture, and graphic arts dating from the Middle Ages to the present.

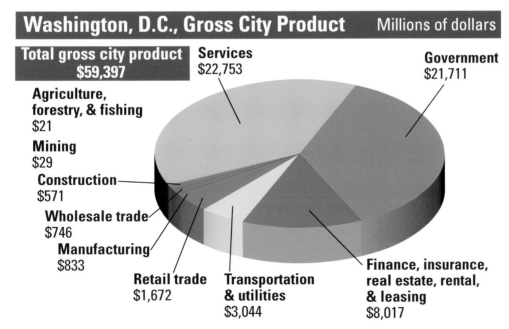

Washington, D.C., Gross City Product — Millions of dollars

Total gross city product $59,397

- **Services** $22,753
- **Government** $21,711
- **Agriculture, forestry, & fishing** $21
- **Mining** $29
- **Construction** $571
- **Wholesale trade** $746
- **Manufacturing** $833
- **Retail trade** $1,672
- **Transportation & utilities** $3,044
- **Finance, insurance, real estate, rental, & leasing** $8,017

Tourism

Few cities in the world have as much to offer the visitor as Washington, D.C. Monuments, historic buildings, world-class museums, and the very fact that it is the seat of government of a superpower have made the capital a destination for tourists from all over the world. An enormous industry has developed to accommodate them. Tourists arrive on planes, travel to hotels in taxis, eat in restaurants, purchase souvenirs, and visit monuments and museums. They have their clothes cleaned, their film developed, and leave the same way they arrived. All of those businesses — the airlines, the taxi companies, the hotels, the restaurants, the companies that produce the food served at the restaurants — are part of the tourism industry of the capital. All of the many people employed by these companies depend on a steady flow of visitors.

By all accounts, the tourism industry is doing very well. Hotels are generally close to full, with occupancy in the year 2000 at 73 percent. Washington, D.C., has more than one hundred hotels, with more than 25,600 rooms. The busiest seasons for tourism are spring and summer, but increasingly, the many organizations that encourage tourism have developed ways to attract year-round visitors. Business and academic conventions are frequently held in the capital, increasing the number of visitors in recent years. The Washington Convention Center, scheduled to open in 2003, should encourage even more companies to hold their conventions in the capital. The $800 million center is located at Mount Vernon Square.

Katherine Graham

Born in 1917, Katherine Graham seemed destined to follow a conservative path: marry a suitable man who could help run the newspaper her father owned, raise children, and remain at home. But when her husband, publisher of the *Washington Post* newspaper, committed suicide in 1963, the woman who described herself as quiet and insecure took charge and turned a mediocre newspaper into one of the best and most powerful daily papers in the world. Graham stood up to political pressure from the White House during the Watergate scandal when the *Post* reported President Nixon's role in covering up a break-in at Democratic party offices. At the time of her death in 2001, Graham was considered one of the most influential people of the twentieth century.

The Private Sector

Besides tourism, most of the businesses in the capital have some connection to the federal government. Many national and international organizations have relocated their headquarters to Washington, D.C. Lobbyists (people who try to influence lawmakers to help a special interest group), lawyers, and accountants are all employed by the various companies and foundations that have moved there as the federal government has become more and more involved with private industry.

▲ Lobbyists, lawyers, and other business people from the United States and around the world visit the Capitol each day Congress is in session.

Washington, D.C., has seen great financial growth in the early years of the twenty-first century. Retail sales have increased steadily and many major national companies have opened stores in the district. The MCI Center, the sports arena that opened in 1997, has brought many people to the downtown area. As a result, many new stores and restaurants have opened. The real estate market, including both commercial (business) and private housing, has grown steadily. In addition to these improvements, Congress approved the formation of the National Capital Revitalization Corporation (NCRC). This corporation provides assistance to district neighborhoods and works to develop businesses in the area. Founded in 2000, the NCRC has begun several projects that will provide jobs for citizens, as well as improve neglected neighborhoods. The NCRC works closely with the mayor's office to decide which projects are most important to the people. Many areas in the city have benefited from this organization's work, including the Southwest Waterfront and more than ten sites throughout the Columbia Heights neighborhood. Planned improvements include building new housing and making efforts to attract businesses to underdeveloped neighborhoods.

Major Airports		
Airport	**Location**	**Passengers per year (2000)**
Washington Dulles International Airport	Loudon County, Virginia	19,971,260
Ronald Reagan Washington National Airport	Arlington County, Virginia	15,724,613

The Struggle for Self-Rule

> The basis of our political system is the right
> of the people to make and to alter their
> constitutions of government.
>
> — *George Washington, farewell address,*
> *September 17, 1796*

From the moment George Washington chose the site of what was to become Washington, D.C., the question of how it was governed and by whom became a cause for concern and, occasionally, controversy. The District was established on land from Virginia and Maryland in 1791, but there were only three thousand people living in the area. Federal law maintained that, to be a state, there must be a minimum of fifty thousand citizens. As a result, the residents of the District continued to vote in their former state, either Maryland or Virginia.

During the ten years before the federal government moved to Washington, D.C., three city commissioners appointed by President Washington governed. In 1801, Congress passed a law that divided the District into two counties, one linked to Maryland and the other linked to Virginia. In 1802, the citizens of the District petitioned Congress for the right to home rule — they wanted to be able to vote for their leaders just like every other citizen in the United States. Congress created a charter that gave Washingtonians the right to vote for a city council that could pass laws and levy a real estate tax, but the highest governing official, the mayor, was to be appointed by the president. This system remained in place for almost seventy years. For three years in the 1870s, Washington had a governor and a council, both appointed by the president. Later, the city returned to the three-commissioner model chosen by George Washington. This form of government lasted until 1967, when Congress granted the city the right to a mayor and a nine-member city council. The president appointed the mayor and the

Elected Posts in the Executive Branch		
Office	Length of Term	Term Limits
Mayor	4 years	none

city council members.

In 1973, Congress passed the Home Rule Act, which finally gave Washington, D.C., the right to vote for its own mayor and council. Voters also choose the advisory neighborhood commissioners, officials who make decisions on basic neighborhood issues. Congress checks the home rule government's power, as it must approve all laws as well as the city budget.

Executive Branch

At the head of the executive branch of city government is the mayor. The mayor of Washington, D.C., serves a four-year term. There is no limit to the number of terms the mayor can serve. Working with the mayor in the executive branch of the city government are five deputy mayors. The deputy mayor, who acts as the city administrator, oversees the other four deputy mayors. The deputy mayor for planning and economic development promotes business and housing in the city. The deputy mayor for operations coordinates public works and transportation. The deputy mayor for children, youth, family, and elders addresses health and social issues. The deputy mayor of public safety and justice works to make the city a safer place for its people. The mayor appoints the deputy mayors, but their appointments must be confirmed by the city council.

▼ Anthony Williams was elected mayor of Washington, D.C., in 1999. He balanced the budget while serving as the city's chief financial officer from 1995 to 1998.

Legislative Branch

The Council of the District of Columbia serves as the lawmaking arm of city government. The council is composed of a chair and four members elected at large — that is, from any part of the city rather than from one particular

ward — and eight other members are from each of the city's eight wards. The council has the right to adopt laws and to approve the district's annual budget as presented by the mayor. Congress reviews all legislation passed by the council before it becomes law, however, and it still controls the budget.

Judicial Branch

Until the Court Reorganization Plan of 1970, the judicial system of the District of Columbia's government had an extremely complicated system of two federal courts, three local courts, and separate appeals courts for each. Under the reorganization plan, the system was divided into a single trial court, the Superior Court of the District of Columbia; a single appeals court, the United States Court of Appeals for the District of Columbia; and a probate court. As in all states, a case would first be heard by the superior court, and, if either party appealed the findings, it could then go on to the court of appeals. The probate court handles the probate of wills and other estate issues.

▲ Dorothy Brizill, executive director of D.C. Watch, a public advocacy group which monitors the District government, talks with reporters outside the District of Columbia Court of Appeals.

Recent Developments in Home Rule

There have been only four elected mayors since the first took office in 1975: Walter Washington (1975–1979), Marion Barry (1979–1991, 1995–1999), Sharon Pratt Kelly (1991–1995), and Anthony Williams (elected 1999). Each mayor faced a multitude of social and economic problems. Financially, the city suffered because it could not tax the many federal properties or tax the income of the many professionals who work in the city but live in the suburbs. The inability of the city to tax federal property was a particularly difficult one. From the very beginning, the District was conceived as the home of the U. S. government, and any building that houses a government office is federal property. As a result, very little of the property within the city generates any tax income. Throughout the 1970s, community activists sought to have Washington, D.C., declared the fifty-first state and at the same time reduce the amount of land that was federal property. This would allow the city to generate more income from taxes, which would alleviate some of its problems. This measure was finally rejected in 1993.

The social problems facing Washington, D.C., were among the worst in the country. The city had a very high unemployment rate during much of the second half of the twentieth century. Infant mortality (the death rate of newborn babies) in poor neighborhoods was twice the national average, and violent crime was on the rise.

Marion Barry was mayor for much of the last quarter of the twentieth century, when the city's crime rate soared, its school system suffered, and the percentage of Washingtonians living at or below poverty level was twice the national average. In 1990, he was arrested on a drug charge. After serving six months in jail, he was elected to the city council in 1992 and elected again as mayor in 1994.

In 1995, the city had a budget deficit, or debt, of $700 million. To keep the city running, Congress set up a board, the Financial Responsibility and Management Assistance Authority, to control the city's finances. In 1997, the federal government began to contribute more money to the city's budget, but in return, Congress demanded the right to choose the city manager. Congress, along with the city manager, controlled the city. In 2001, with the city operating on a balanced budget, Congress gave control of the city back to the mayor and the city council.

The District's First Mayor

Walter Washington, the first mayor of Washington, D.C., was born in upstate New York. After graduating from Howard University in 1948, he attended Howard Law School, where he encountered African-American lawyers such as Thurgood Marshall, who would later become a Supreme Court justice. After working in the Kennedy administration, Washington was appointed commissioner of Washington, D.C., by President Lyndon Johnson in 1967. When Congress allowed the city to elect its own government in 1975, Washington was elected mayor. Although he had been leading the city since 1967, he served only one four-year term as mayor.

▶ President Clinton, surrounded by Washington, D.C., and government officials, signs the District of Columbia's 1998 budget into law. The federal government provides funding to the city to help it meet its financial obligations.

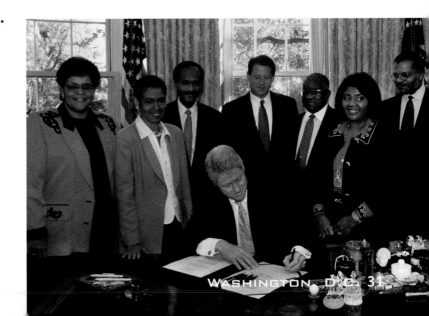

Music and Museums

> To found at Washington, under the name of the Smithsonian Institution, an establishment for the increase and diffusion of knowledge among men.
>
> — *James Smithson, bequest to found the Smithsonian Institution, 1829*

DID YOU KNOW?

One of the most commonly planted shrubs around federal buildings in Washington, D.C., is the American yew, which has the botanical name of *Taxus canadensis*.

There is more to see in Washington, D.C., than a visitor could manage in a month of walking tours, but that hasn't stopped the more than twenty million visitors a year from trying. L'Enfant's careful planning of the city and the many additions of the last two centuries have made Washington, D.C., one of the most beautiful cities in the nation.

Easily one of the most famous houses in the world, the White House has been the president's home for over two hundred years. Visitors can tour several rooms, among them the State Dining Room and the East Room. Every year, over one million people pay a call to this historic home, which underwent a major restoration headed by First Lady Jacqueline Kennedy in the 1960s.

The Capitol, recognizable by its enormous, stately dome, is where the House of Representatives and the Senate meet to create the laws that govern the country. The building, with 540 rooms and a rotunda (circular room) under the dome that measures 96 feet (about 29 m) in diameter, is an impressive symbol of the important work that is done there, just as William Thornton, the original architect, intended.

▼ Work on the U.S. Capitol began in 1793. In 1800, the Senate and House of Representatives began meeting in the building. Since then, additions have more than doubled its size.

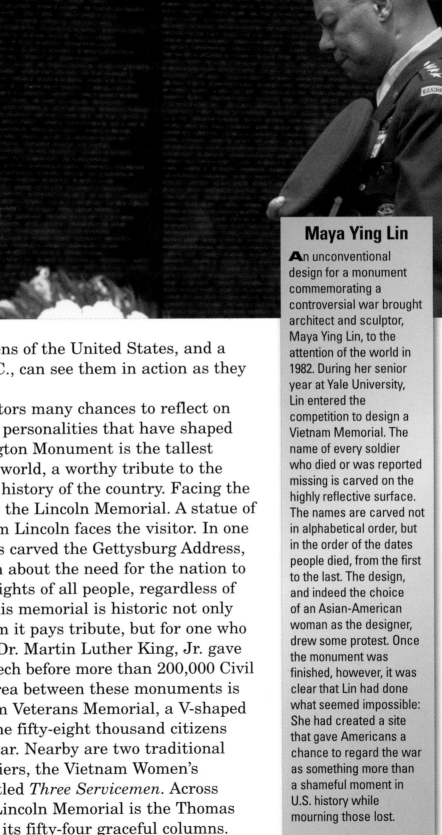

General Colin Powell stands in front of the polished black granite of the Vietnam Veterans Memorial.

Next to the Capitol is the Supreme Court building, where the nine Supreme Court justices review the laws of the United States and how they are applied. Hearing an average of five hundred cases a year, the justices have an awesome responsibility to the citizens of the United States, and a visitor to Washington, D.C., can see them in action as they fulfill it.

Washington offers visitors many chances to reflect on the important events and personalities that have shaped this country. The Washington Monument is the tallest masonry structure in the world, a worthy tribute to the man who towers over the history of the country. Facing the Washington Monument is the Lincoln Memorial. A statue of a seated, pensive Abraham Lincoln faces the visitor. In one of two marble chambers is carved the Gettysburg Address, his simple, moving speech about the need for the nation to continue to fight for the rights of all people, regardless of color, in the Civil War. This memorial is historic not only for the great man to whom it pays tribute, but for one who came after: On its steps, Dr. Martin Luther King, Jr. gave his "I Have a Dream" speech before more than 200,000 Civil Rights supporters. The area between these monuments is dominated by the Vietnam Veterans Memorial, a V-shaped black granite tribute to the fifty-eight thousand citizens killed or missing in the war. Nearby are two traditional monuments to fallen soldiers, the Vietnam Women's Memorial and a statue titled *Three Servicemen*. Across the tidal basin from the Lincoln Memorial is the Thomas Jefferson Memorial, with its fifty-four graceful columns.

Maya Ying Lin

An unconventional design for a monument commemorating a controversial war brought architect and sculptor, Maya Ying Lin, to the attention of the world in 1982. During her senior year at Yale University, Lin entered the competition to design a Vietnam Memorial. The name of every soldier who died or was reported missing is carved on the highly reflective surface. The names are carved not in alphabetical order, but in the order of the dates people died, from the first to the last. The design, and indeed the choice of an Asian-American woman as the designer, drew some protest. Once the monument was finished, however, it was clear that Lin had done what seemed impossible: She had created a site that gave Americans a chance to regard the war as something more than a shameful moment in U.S. history while mourning those lost.

Libraries and Museums

The Library of Congress is the world's largest library. Founded in 1800, but not completed until 1897, it lost many books in the fire set by the British during the siege of Washington in the War of 1812. One of the earliest and most important acquisitions of the library was the purchase of Thomas Jefferson's personal library. Today, the library acquires some four hundred items every hour.

The Smithsonian Institution is actually a group of sixteen museums and galleries, as well as performing arts centers and laboratories, but it is best known for its collections. Among the highlights is the Hope diamond, the world's largest blue diamond, which formerly belonged to Marie Antoinette, queen of France in the eighteenth century. The National Zoological Park, in Rock Creek Park, is also part of the Smithsonian; it is home to a new baby Asian elephant named Kandula, as well as giant pandas, sea lions, and Mexican wolves.

The National Gallery of Art is near the Capitol. In 1937, philanthropist Andrew Mellon donated his art collection

▲ The Thomas Jefferson building of the Library of Congress was renovated for more than ten years and reopened in 1997 for its hundredth birthday.

DID YOU KNOW?

The peak of the Washington Monument isn't stone like the rest of the structure. It is made of aluminum, which was very expensive when the monument was completed in 1884.

and millions of dollars to create this museum. The East Building of the museum, designed by architect I. M. Pei and completed in 1978, now houses works by artists such as Alexander Calder and Pablo Picasso.

Communications

Washington, D.C., has two major daily newspapers, the *Washington Post* and the *Washington Times*. Of the two, the *Post* is the more liberal. It has been an internationally recognized paper since the 1970s. The paper was awarded the 1973 Pulitzer Prize for public service for its reporting of the Watergate break-in and the Nixon administration's role in it. The *Times*, which was founded in 1982, has gained a reputation as a conservative newspaper. In addition to the two daily newspapers, *The Hill* is a weekly newspaper founded in 1994 to report exclusively on Congress, its decisions, and their effect on the American people.

Music and Theater

Washington, D.C., offers performances of live music and theater throughout the year. Founded in 1931, the National Symphony Orchestra presents approximately 175 concerts each year at the Kennedy Center. The orchestra's one hundred musicians perform year-round, including outdoor concerts on the West Lawn of the U.S. Capitol. The

▼ **The National Symphony Orchestra is composed of one hundred musicians who give 175 performances annually.**

Washington Opera, founded in 1956, is currently led by
Placido Domingo, an opera star. Like the National Symphony
Orchestra, the Washington Opera stages its performances at
the Kennedy Center. The National Theatre, which opened in
1835, is Washington's oldest cultural institution. An 1850
appearance by soprano Jenny Lind ("The Swedish
Nightingale"), created such a stir that Congress adjourned
and police kept the crowd in order. More recent stars include
Laurence Olivier, Ethel Merman, and Sarah Bernhardt.

There are many venues for popular music as well,
including several that feature go-go, a style of dance music
that is unique to Washington, D.C. Go-go music began in the
1960s and blends African percussion, funk rhythms, and rap-
style vocals. Go-go bands play at many clubs in the city. The
bands typically have nine or ten members, including several
percussionists. Although many go-go bands have recorded
their music, as a style it has never really reached beyond the
city. There are also many jazz clubs in the area, some of which
attract well-known performers such as Wynton Marsalis and
Eartha Kitt.

▲ Named after
President Kennedy,
the Kennedy Center
has several different
theaters, including a
children's theater.

Sports

Politics may be the most popular topic of conversation
in Washington, D.C., but sports must be a close second.
Although the city has four professional sports teams,

Sport	Team	Home
Football (NFL)	Washington Redskins	FedEx Field
Basketball (NBA)	Washington Wizards	MCI Center
Basketball (WNBA)	Washington Mystics	MCI Center
Hockey (NHL)	Washington Capitals	MCI Center

Washingtonians are most passionate about their football team, the Washington Redskins. On October 25, 2002, the team celebrated its seventieth anniversary. In those seventy years, the Redskins won three Super Bowls. One of the team's best-known players is Ken Houston, who played from 1973 to 1980. The Redskins had to trade five players for him. Houston was inducted into the Pro Football Hall of Fame in 1986. The Washington Wizards are the capital's professional basketball team. Playing under their former name, the Bullets, the Wizards won the National Basketball Association (NBA) championship in 1978, led by Wes Unseld and Elvin Hayes. The Women's National Basketball Association (WNBA) is represented by the Washington Mystics. The Washington Capitals, formed in 1974, represent Washington, D.C., in the National Hockey League.

Washingtonians are justifiably proud of their new sports center, the MCI Center in downtown Washington. Built in 1997, this $200 million arena can accommodate twenty thousand fans. The MCI Center offers many kinds of events, such as sports competitions, music concerts, and family shows. One interesting feature of this striking arena is the large expanses of glass that allow a view of the city from the seats inside. From the highest seats in the arena, ticket holders can see the National Portrait Gallery and the National Museum of American Art. Inside, the center has four levels of comfortable seating, large video screens, and food service.

▶ Doug Williams — despite having root canal surgery that morning, and hurting his knee in the first quarter — turned in one of the greatest Super Bowl performances of all time in 1988.

Washington, D.C., Greats

It's been over forty years since Washington, D.C., had a professional baseball team, the Washington Senators. One of their most famous players, "Goose" Goslin, hit seven home runs in his first sixteen World Series games. In the 1924 World Series, Goslin had eleven hits and three home runs, leading to Washington's seven-game victory over the New York Giants. Goslin compiled a lifetime batting average of .316.

No football fan watching Super Bowl XXII in 1988 can forget Doug Williams and his heroic second quarter. He exploded for 228 yards and a record four touchdowns. His performance that day won him the Most Valuable Player Award for Super Bowl XXII. Williams retired from football two years later due to a back injury.

Great Washingtonians

> My observation is that whenever one person is found adequate to the discharge of a duty . . . it is worse executed by two persons, and scarcely done at all if three or more are employed therein.
>
> — *George Washington*

Following are only a few of the thousands of people who were born, died, or spent much of their lives in Washington, D.C., and made extraordinary contributions to the city and the nation.

THOMAS JEFFERSON
U.S. PRESIDENT

BORN: *April 13, 1743, Albemarle County, VA*
DIED: *July 4, 1826, near Charlottesville, VA*

A brilliant politician, a gifted architect, and an articulate writer, Thomas Jefferson is one of the most accomplished men of all time. At thirty-three years of age, he wrote the Declaration of Independence in two sittings, on June 11 and June 28, 1776. In 1785, he was appointed the minister to France, where he developed sympathy for the French Revolution. Back in the United States, Jefferson grew wary of a strong central government and helped organize a new political party that emphasized liberty. Jefferson was elected president in 1800 and served two terms from 1801 to 1809, when he retired to his home, Monticello. He spent his final years helping to found the University of Virginia.

CLARA BARTON
RED CROSS PRESIDENT

BORN: *December 25, 1821, Oxford, MA*
DIED: *April 12, 1912, Glen Echo, MD*

Clara Barton's first career was as a schoolteacher in Massachusetts and New Jersey. An early advocate of women's rights, Barton left her job when her school gave a job she deserved to a man. During the Civil War, she nursed wounded soldiers and encouraged businesses to donate much-needed medical supplies. After the war, she traveled to Europe, where she learned about the Red Cross, an organization founded to help people in times of war and natural disasters. In 1881, Barton was named the first president of the American Red Cross. She lived and worked in Washington, D.C., until she retired in 1904.

ALEXANDER GRAHAM BELL
INVENTOR

BORN: *March 3, 1847, Edinburgh, Scotland*
DIED: *August 2, 1922, Baddeck, Nova Scotia*

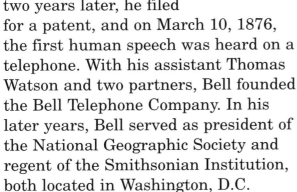

After completing his education in London, Alexander Graham Bell moved to Boston, Massachusetts, and began teaching deaf children. In 1874, while experimenting at the Massachusetts Institute of Technology, Bell came up with the basic idea of the telephone. Less than two years later, he filed for a patent, and on March 10, 1876, the first human speech was heard on a telephone. With his assistant Thomas Watson and two partners, Bell founded the Bell Telephone Company. In his later years, Bell served as president of the National Geographic Society and regent of the Smithsonian Institution, both located in Washington, D.C.

FRANCES HODGSON BURNETT
AUTHOR

BORN: *November 24, 1849, Manchester, England*
DIED: *October 29, 1924, Plandome, NY*

Frances Hodgson Burnett's father died when she was five, and she moved with her mother, two brothers, and two sisters to Tennessee when she was sixteen, where the family struggled

to make a living. At the age of twenty-three, she had her first real publishing success with "Surly Tim's Trouble," published in *Scribner's* magazine. She had a gift for writing stories that used the speech of her native Lancashire, England, in a fresh way, and she was soon in demand as a writer. After marrying in 1873 and settling in Washington, D.C., Burnett had her greatest successes with the novels *Little Lord Fauntleroy* (1886), *A Little Princess* (1905), and *The Secret Garden* (1911).

JOHN PHILIP SOUSA
COMPOSER

BORN: *November 6, 1854, Washington, D.C.*
DIED: *March 6, 1932, Reading, PA*

John Philip Sousa started his career as an apprentice musician in the Marine Corps at the age of thirteen, following in the steps of his father, who had been a member since the Civil War. At the age of twenty-five, Sousa became the leader of the Marine Band. He composed about 140 miltary marches, many of which remain familiar today. His band became known for its innovative musical techniques. The people of Washington, among them President

Hayes, looked forward to its performance. Sousa performed before five presidents: Hayes, Garfield, Arthur, Cleveland, and Harrison. In 1892, Sousa resigned from the Marines to start his own band, the first to tour the world.

ALICE ROOSEVELT LONGWORTH
SOCIAL ICON

BORN: *February 12, 1884, New York, NY*
DIED: *February 20, 1980, Washington, D.C.*

In her youth, Alice Roosevelt Longworth was known primarily for being the irreverent daughter of President Theodore Roosevelt. Over the course of her ninety-six years, her wit, caustic sense of humor, and intelligence made her an even more notable figure. As a White House child with an independent personality, she smoked on the roof of the White House when her father forbade her from smoking inside. At twenty-two years of age, she married Ohio Congressman Nicholas Longworth, a man who would one day be Speaker of the House. Her quotations have been widely circulated over the years, often to the dismay of those she was talking about. Of President Calvin Coolidge (1923–1929) she said, "It looks as though he was weaned on a pickle." When Joseph McCarthy, the senator known for his false accusations of communism, called her by her first name, she responded by saying: "My maid can call me Alice, and the man who collects my trash can call me Alice, but you, Senator McCarthy, can call me Mrs. Longworth." The woman who called herself "a walking Washington monument" met every president from Benjamin Harrison (1889–1893) to Jimmy Carter (1977–1981), and her outlook on human nature is best remembered by a saying she had stitched onto a pillow in her living room: "If you haven't got anything good to say about anybody, come sit next to me."

JOHN FOSTER DULLES
STATESMAN

BORN: *February 25, 1888, Washington, D.C.*
DIED: *May 24, 1959, Washington, D.C.*

The grandson of the secretary of state under President Harrison, John Foster Dulles discovered an interest in foreign policy when he attended the second Hague Peace Conference with his grandfather in 1907. He graduated from Princeton University the following year and attended George Washington University Law School. After working as a lawyer in New York City, Dulles took an army commission during World War I. Later, he served as a delegate to the United Nations General Assembly before taking the most important job of his career, secretary of state under President Eisenhower. He resigned this position in 1959 when he was diagnosed with cancer. He died five weeks later.

J. EDGAR HOOVER
DIRECTOR OF THE F.B.I.

BORN: *January 1, 1895, Washington, D.C.*
DIED: *May 2, 1972, Washington, D.C.*

J. Edgar Hoover was the youngest of four children. He worked at the Library of Congress while attending George Washington University and George Washington University School of

Law. When he graduated, he went to work in the Justice Department. He would never leave. For the next fifty-five years, Hoover dedicated his life to investigating crime in this country. While some of his efforts were admirable, many of them, including his investigation into the personal life of Martin Luther King, Jr., amounted to little more than personal grudges. He ran the Federal Bureau of Investigation with an iron hand for over fifty years. He died at home at the age of seventy-seven.

EDWARD "DUKE" ELLINGTON
MUSICIAN

BORN: *April 25, 1899, Washington, D.C.*
DIED: *May 24, 1974, New York, NY*

Nicknamed "Duke" for his cool, regal elegance, Edward Ellington named his first orchestra "The Washingtonians." His music helped usher in the Jazz Age of the 1920s. The famous Harlem nightclub — the Cotton Club — hired Ellington and his orchestra as the house band in 1927. Weekly radio broadcasts from the club made him famous, and by the time he left the club in 1931, his band was in demand all over the United States and Europe. His music shifted from the hot jazz of the 1920s to the swing music of the 1930s, but it always had an identifiable elegance that was the Duke's signature style. Songs such as "Take the 'A' Train" and "Mood Indigo" have become classics in the music world.

SANDRA DAY O'CONNOR
SUPREME COURT JUSTICE

BORN: *March 26, 1930, El Paso, TX*

Born and raised on her family's cattle ranch, O'Connor first became interested in law when her family was involved in a legal dispute over their land. She attended Stanford University and Stanford University Law School. As an Arizona assistant attorney general, she was known as conservative and hardworking. She served in the Arizona state senate from 1969 to 1975 and was senate majority leader from 1974 to 1975. In 1981, President Ronald Reagan appointed O'Connor to the U.S. Supreme Court. She was the first female Supreme Court justice. Her legal decisions are considered practical and centrist.

JESSE JACKSON
CIVIL RIGHTS LEADER

BORN: *October 8, 1941, Greenville, SC*

On a football scholarship at the University of Illinois, Jesse Jackson encountered racial discrimination, just as he had growing up in the South. He began working in the Civil Rights Movement. After Martin Luther King, Jr. was assassinated in 1968, Jackson seemed a natural successor to lead the Civil Rights movement. In 1984, he ran for the Democratic nomination for president against Walter Mondale. Although he lost, the campaign brought him even more recognition. Jackson campaigned for the Democratic nomination in 1988, but lost again. In 2000, President Clinton awarded Jackson the Presidential Medal of Freedom, the highest honor available to civilians.

Washington, D.C.

History At-A-Glance

1790
Congress declares that the new capital will be built on land in the Potomac region.

1791
Pierre-Charles L'Enfant is chosen by President Washington to design the city.

1792
Construction begins on the president's house.

1793
Construction begins on the U.S. Capitol.

1802
The new city is designated the nation's capital, and federal employees move in.

1802
The new capital is named the City of Washington.

1814
British troops burn the president's house and the Capitol.

1860
Lincoln is elected president.

1862
Slavery is declared illegal in Washington, D.C., eight months before Lincoln's Emancipation Proclamation.

1865
Lincoln is assassinated.

1867
Howard University opens.

1881
Clara Barton is named first president of the American Red Cross.

1600   **1700**   **1800**

1492
Christopher Columbus comes to New World.

1607
Capt. John Smith and three ships land on Virginia coast and start first English settlement in New World — Jamestown.

1754–63
French and Indian War.

1773
Boston Tea Party.

1776
Declaration of Independence adopted July 4.

1777
Articles of Confederation adopted by Continental Congress.

1787
U.S. Constitution written.

1812–14
War of 1812.

United States

History At-A-Glance

1888
Washington Monument is opened to the public.

1937
Andrew Mellon donates his art collection to create the National Gallery of Art.

1963
John F. Kennedy is buried in Arlington National Cemetery.

1974
Nixon resigns under suspicion of his role in the Watergate break-in.

1994
Marion Barry is re-elected as mayor of Washington, D.C..

1897
The Library of Congress is completed.

1922
The Lincoln Memorial is completed.

1963
Martin Luther King, Jr. gives his "I Have a Dream" speech.

1970
The judical system of the district is reorganized.

1981
Sandra Day O'Connor is the first woman appointed to the U.S. Supreme Court.

2001
Congress returns control of the district to the mayor and city council.

1800   **1900**   **2000**

1848
Gold discovered in California draws eighty thousand prospectors in the 1849 Gold Rush.

1869
Transcontinental railroad completed.

1929
Stock market crash ushers in Great Depression.

1950–53
U.S. fights in the Korean War.

2000
George W. Bush wins the closest presidential election in history.

1917–18
U.S. involvement in World War I.

1941–45
U.S. involvement in World War II.

1964–73
U.S. involvement in Vietnam War.

1861–65
Civil War.

2001
A terrorist attack in which four hijacked airliners crash into New York City's World Trade Center, the Pentagon, and farmland in western Pennsylvania leaves thousands dead or injured.

▼ **The chamber of the House of Representatives in the Capitol as it appeared in 1868.**

Festivals and Fun for All

Check web site for exact date and directions.

The Capital Jazz Fest

Join the nation's hippest jazz musicians in June for this annual celebration of jazz.
www.capitaljazzfest.com

Capitol Holiday Tree Lighting

The U.S. Congress holds its own tree-lighting ceremony every year on the west lawn of the Capitol. Watch as the speaker of the house flips the switch at this holiday event.
www.capitolholidaytree2002.com

D.C. Blues Festival

This annual celebration of blues music is for young and old fans of this classic Southern music.
www.dcblues.org

Fiesta Musical

This Latin music festival is held each fall at the National Zoo.
www.fonz.org/calendar.htm

Filmfest DC

This international event features an opening night gala, more than eighty feature film premieres, and awards in categories ranging from best children's film to best documentary.
www.filmfestdc.org

The Folklore Society Minifestival

Join area folklore lovers in this February celebration of music, dance, and stories. This event draws crowds from up and down the eastern seaboard.
www.fsgw.org

For Sisters Only

This two-day expo for African-American women and girls celebrates their unique culture and many contributions to American life.
www.washington.org

Frederick Douglass Birthday Tribute

Celebrate the February birthday of this great leader, born in 1817, at his National Historic Site.
www.washington.org

Kwanzaa Celebration at the Smithsonian

This joyous celebration of the festival of Kwanzaa features music, dance, games, and storytelling. The different events take place at various Smithsonian museums, among them the National Museum of African American Art, the National Museum of Natural History, and the Anacostia Museum and Center for African American History and Culture.
www.smithsonian.org

The National Capital Barbecue Battle

Enjoy live shows, games, rides, and, of course, great barbecue at this June family festival.
www.barbecuebattle.com/attraction.htm

The National Cherry Blossom Festival

Short of going to Japan, there is no better place to see cherry trees in bloom than Washington, D.C., in the spring.
www.nationalcherryblossomfestival.org

The Pageant of Peace Tree Lighting Ceremony

Join the president, the first lady, and one very large tree at Christmas as a way to start the season.
www.whitehouse.gov/president/holiday/tree

The Washington Antiquarian Book Fair

Thousands of rare books, new books, drawings, and sheet music attract book lovers of all ages.
www.wabf.com

The Washington Craft Show

Join the nation's top craft experts as they demonstrate their skills at this craft show.
www.craftsamericashows.com/washington_info.htm

The White House Easter Egg Roll

Historians believe that First Lady Dolley Madison was the first to have local kids join her at Easter for fun, but she held her party at the Capitol. Since 1878, the White House has been home to this family tradition.
www.whitehouse.gov/history/tours/easter.html

▶ The First Family is not the only one to enjoy a holiday tree-lighting ceremony. Congress and the Speaker of the House have started their own Christmas tradition with their own tree on the lawn of the Capitol.

Books

Brill, Marlene Targ. *Building the Capital City (Cornerstones of Freedom)*. Danbury: Children's Press, 1996. An interesting guide to the creation of the important buildings in the capital.

Doherty, Craig, and Katherine Doherty. *The Washington Monument (Building America)*. Farmington Hills: Blackbirch Marketing, 1995. Full-color photographs and simple text tell the story of how this monument was built.

Harness, Cheryl. *Ghosts of the White House*. New York: Simon and Schuster, 1998. A collection of tales from people who think the White House is haunted.

Levey, Jane Freundel, Patricia K. Kummer, and Capstone Press Geography Department. *Washington, D.C. (One Nation)*. Minnetonka: Bridgestone Books, 1998. The story of the city of Washington, D.C., and its people.

Santella, Andrew. *The Capitol (Cornerstones of Freedom)*. Danbury: Children's Press, 1995. Learn more about Washington, D.C., its buildings, and its history.

Wilson, Jon. *The White House: 1600 Pennsylvania Avenue*. Chanhasser: Child's World, 1998. Read about one of the most famous houses in the world.

Web Sites

▶ Official city web site
www.washingtondc.gov

▶ Historical Society of Washington, D.C.
www.hswdc.org

▶ The White House web site
www.whitehouse.gov

▶ United States Senate web site
www.senate.gov

▶ United States House of Representatives web site
www.house.gov